WHITE WATER THRILLS

Henry Billings and Melissa Billings

Published in association with The Basic Skills Agency

Hodder & Stoughton

A MEMBER OF THE HODDER HEADLINE

Acknowledgements

Cover: Dan Smith/Allsport.

Photos: pp. 2, 5, 16, 19, 23 © Action-Plus Photographic; p. 9 Life File; p. 12 © Allsport; p. 26 © Corbis.

Orders: please contact Bookpoint Ltd, 130 Milton Park, Abingdon, Oxon OX14 4SB. Telephone: (44) 01235 400414, Fax: (44) 01235 400454. Lines are open 9.00–6.00, Monday to Saturday, with a 24-hour message answering service. Email address: orders@bookpoint.co.uk

British Library Cataloguing in Publication Data
A catalogue record for this title is available from The British Library

ISBN 0 340 74776 5

Published by Jamestown Publishers,
a division of NTC/Contemporary Publishing Group, Inc.

Copyright © 1996 by NTC/Contemporary Publishing Group, Inc.

First published 1999 by Hodder & Stoughton Educational Publishers.
Impression number   10 9 8 7 6 5 4 3 2
Year   2004 2003 2002 2001

Typeset by Fakenham Photosetting Ltd, Fakenham, Norfolk.
Printed in Great Britain for Hodder & Stoughton Educational, a division of Hodder Headline Plc, 338 Euston Road, London NW1 3BH by The Bath Press, Bath

You can go to a theme park
and ride a log flume.
It's safe and lots of fun.
But a log flume is the same ride
over and over again.
If you want to try something different,
try white water rafting.
A white water ride is never the same twice.
New thrills and dangers lie downstream
every time you run the rapids.

White water rivers can be wild.

White water means river rapids.
The water becomes a foamy white
when it swirls over and around the rocks.
All rapids are called white water.
But not all white water rivers are the same.
Some are quite calm; others are really wild.
Rafters need to know what they are facing.

A gentle-looking river
can turn into a beast around the next bend.
So all rivers are rated,
based on how hard they are to travel down.

The most common rating system
uses Roman numerals from I to VI.
A Class I* river is wide
with a few small waves.
It's not much more exciting
than a splash in an old bath.

* Class I means Class 1

Some rivers may seem gentle.

A Class III* river is much more difficult.
It has rocks and waves
up to one metre high.
You can expect to get wet running the rapids
of a Class III river.

If you move up to a Class V* river,
you will face violent rapids with no breaks.
You can get killed on a Class V river.

* Class III means Class 3
* Class V means Class 5

A Class VI* river is even worse.
It's a real hair-raiser.
All kinds of dangers await you there.
Anyone who takes on a Class VI river
must be two things –
an expert and a daredevil.

* Class VI means Class 6

A few rivers have sections
that are too dangerous.
These Class VII* rivers
can't be rafted by anyone.

* Class VII means Class 7

Some rivers have sections
too dangerous to raft.

Rivers change all the time.
A heavy rain can turn a Class III river
into a Class V or even a Class VI.
Some rivers can be run only in the spring
after the snow melts.
The rest of the time
there just isn't enough water in them.

Rivers are like magnets for thrill seekers.
Some people run the rapids in canoes.
Others use one-person kayaks.
Still others choose five-metre rubber rafts.
The rafts have one big advantage.
They can stay afloat on rivers
that would sink a canoe or kayak.

Running the rapids in a canoe.

One of the top ten white water rivers
in the world is the Gauley River.
It runs through West Virginia in the USA.
The Gauley is a rafter's dream...
or if you're not careful – a nightmare.
It has 28 miles of heart-pounding rapids.

Each set of rapids has its own name.
Some give fair warning to rafters.
One is called Pure Screaming Hell.
There are also Lost Paddle, Heaven Help Us
and Pillow Rock.
One river guide described Pillow Rock as

Fifteen seconds of uncontrolled violence.

Clearly, white water rafting
is not for the meek.
Dangers lurk everywhere.
There is something called a keeper
which is like a whirlpool.
It is created when water rushes
over a huge rock with a steep face.

Water rushing over a rock
can create a whirlpool.

A keeper has enough water power to trap,
or keep, a boat for days.
Imagine what it could do to a person!
Keepers cause more drownings
on white water rapids
than any other hazard.

There are other dangers as well.
There are waterfalls, fallen tree trunks
and sharp boulders.
Any one of these can cause disaster.
And no rafter wants to be caught
in a Colorado sandwich.
That can happen when a raft hits a big wave.
The front and back of the raft
are folded up towards the centre.
Anyone in the middle
is lunch meat in a raft sandwich.

A raft hits a big wave.

Most rafters know the risks.
And they are willing to take them.
But they also do what they can
to cut down the dangers.
They carry at least 16 metres of strong rope
for towing.
They often wear wetsuits and life jackets
in case they get thrown into the water.
And they wear helmets in case they hit
a rock when they fall overboard.

Rafters also wear waterproof shoes.
Some people want to take their shoes off
as soon as they get wet.
Wet shoes are uncomfortable.
And they worry that wearing shoes
will make it harder to swim
if they fall into the water.
But taking off their shoes
would be a mistake.
Shoes protect the rafters' feet
from the rocks.

Look at it this way:
if you end up in the river,
you can't swim anyway.
The current is just too strong.
All you can do is float on your back
with your feet pointed down the river.

Shoes are important if you fall in.

You'll need your feet
to help steer around the rocks.
If you're wearing shoes,
your feet won't get cut badly.
And when you finally reach dry land,
you'll be glad you're wearing shoes.
It might be a long walk home
over very rocky ground!

Every year, thousands of people
enjoy white water rafting.
But sometimes the sport is deadly.
In the summer of 1987
there were four accidents
in British Columbia,
in the West of Canada.
Twelve rafters died in eight weeks.

Rafting in Western Canada.

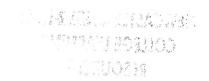

The rivers in that part of Canada
are filled by melting snow.
They are very cold.
Five of the dead rafters
were American businessmen
looking for a thrill.
On 1 August,
they went on the wild Chilko River
without wetsuits.
A huge wave knocked them out of their raft.
The men died in the icy water.

So to enjoy the sport,
you must respect the power of the river.
That means being as careful as possible.
But no extreme sport is completely safe.
The owner of the rafting company
on the Gauley River
warns his customers about the risks.
He and his guides
make sure people know
what they are doing.
He says

We never say rafting is safe.